2

Last Words of the Wise Old Paratrooper by Robin Horsfall.

www.robinhorsfall.co.uk

© 2019 Robin Horsfall

All rights reserved. No portion of this book may be reproduced in any form without permission from the publisher, except as permitted by U.K. copyright law.

Cover by Ernie McGookin.

ISBN: 9781080307784

4

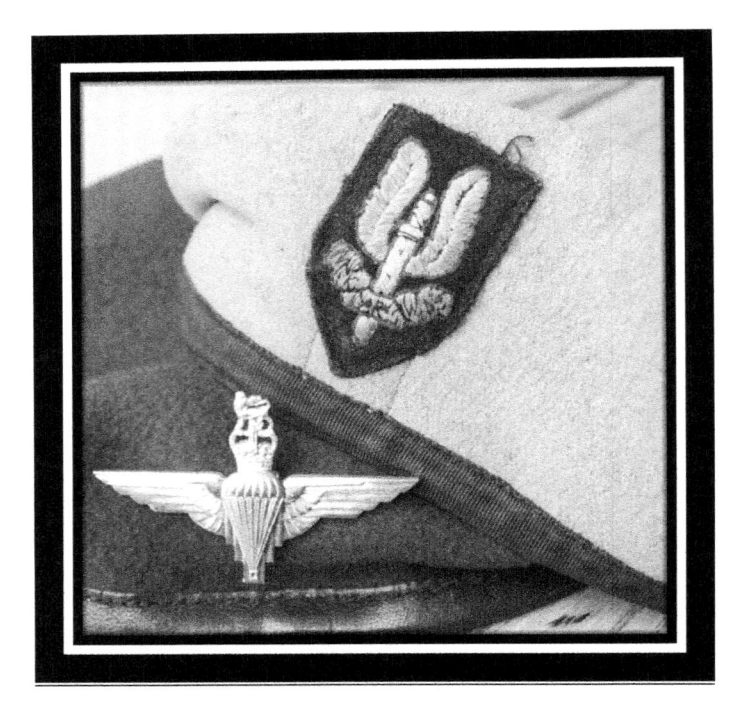

# LAST WORDS OF THE WISE OLD PARATROOPER

# ROBIN HORSFALL

TO ALL MY DEPARTED COMRADES.

NEVER FORGOTTEN.

7

[1] Photo. Heather Horsfall

# The Author

Robin Horsfall was a soldier from the age of fifteen up to the age of thirty-two. He served with the Parachute Regiment, the SAS, The Sultans of Oman's Armed Forces, The Army of Sri Lanka and was a Major in 'Frelimo' The Army of Mozambique. He studied Karate for most of his adult life achieving the rank of 6$^{th}$ Dan Black Belt until in 2011 a neck fracture halted his career. During his recovery he went to Surrey University and studied English literature and creative writing graduating in 2016. Married since 1981 this father of five and grandfather of twelve started posting *'The Sayings of the Wise Old Paratrooper'* on Facebook and later decided to collate them along with his short stories and poetry into this collection. This is the third book in the trilogy.

# Last Words of The Wise Old Paratrooper.

## OMG a QSM

In 1982 Taff was the Quartermaster Sergeant (QMS) of 22 SAS. All our stores and supplies were his responsibility. There are two ways to regard people responsible for material requirements. One is as store men and the other as supply men. The first want to store material and the second want to supply it. The SAS had a reputation for supplying not storing the men's needs.

The Army of course needed to ensure that units did not waste material so they imposed strict rules about exchange of old kit and payment for lost kit. Another measure that they put in place was to award a British Empire Medal to any QMS that met his targets and didn't 'waste' army property.

We were at war, Argentina had invaded the Falkland Islands and our staging post on the eight thousand mile supply line was Ascension Island in middle of the Atlantic Ocean. Hardware was flown down at huge expense to prepare and 'supply' the Army, Navy and Airforce.

The Milan anti-tank guided missile had recently been introduced to the army. Before we left the UK, B Squadron had sent three men, (including me) on a course to learn how to use these hand held weapons. In consideration for our novice standing as Milan Operators four training missiles were allocated to us for practise while we were on Ascension, - training missiles did not have an explosive warhead.

The squadron gathered at the missile ranges for a demonstration of the range and accuracy of the missiles. Each operator fired a missile apiece and we all hit our targets out as far as nearly 2000 metres. The troops were impressed. There were four training missiles and only three operators. Being good at arithmetic, I piped up and said 'Okay we'll draw straws to see who gets the last shot.' The voice of Taff roared from behind me. 'No you're not' he said 'you've had one each. That one's going back to the UK' and in spite of our protests that's what happened to it.

I think he got his medal.

15

***

'If you are prepared to say something then be prepared to do something.'

Who Dares Shares!

'Ensure you have some moral authority before you criticise others.'

'Not being a capitalist does not automatically make you a communist.'

***

***

'At some point in life your ambitions should have become achievements.'

'It's hard to appreciate life when you feel like shit!'

'Don't look down on those who don't know, look down on those who don't want to know.'

***

***

'When you are unkind to a disabled or disadvantaged person just pause for a moment and think. No one can change the brain, body or face they are born with.

'Cruelty is the weapon of cowards and fools.'

***

18

## Solo Soldier

I wasn't allowed to whine so I stopped whining

I wasn't allowed to run so I stopped running

I didn't get any help so I helped myself

No one picked me up so I stopped going down

No one befriended me so I lived without friends

No one lent me money so I managed my funds

No one paid me when I was sick so I worked

Don't whine, don't run away, don't frown

Help yourself, choose your friends, have no debt and

Never let the bastards get you down!

***

'If you don't want to be involved in politics make sure that you can solve all of your problems by yourself.'

Dear God why didn't you make men telepathic too?

Dysfunctional people should be part of our communities and should be helped and tolerated not beaten and abused. Give them a smile, chastise the ignorant bullies and set a good example.

***

\*\*\*

Many mentally disabled people have a sad history that has contributed to their problems. The death or suicide of a loved one, a traumatic injury or just a sensitive nature.

If you let people treat you as though you are stupid – perhaps you are.

\*\*\*

22

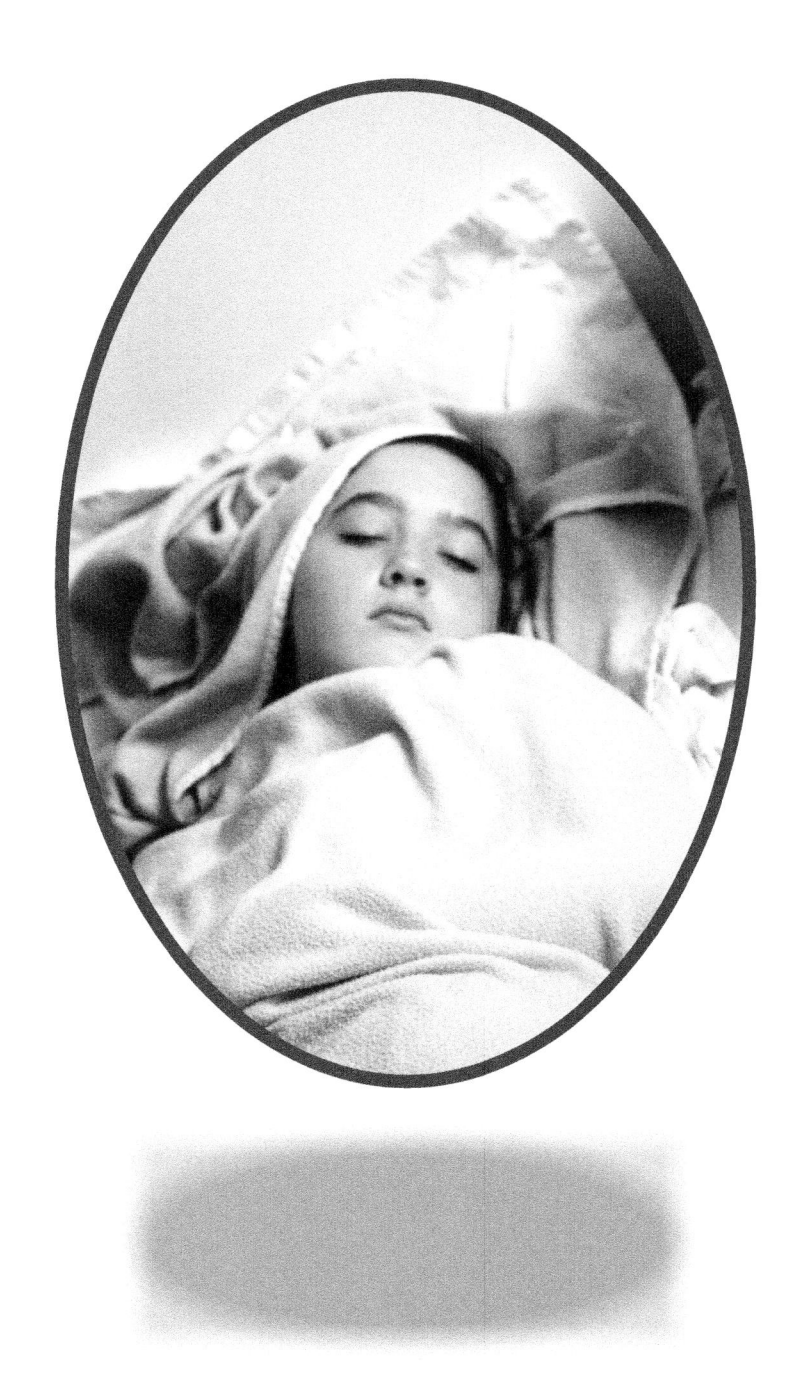

## Time for Bed.

My earliest memory must have been before my third birthday. My mum would say 'It's nearly time for bed' so I would curl up on the chair and close my eyes pretending that I was already asleep.

A few minutes later I would feel my mother's strong arms lift me up and hold me close to her breast. I felt warm and safe knowing that I was going to bed. She would turn and walk towards the stairs in the corner of the room. I felt the gentle, bouncy change of weight as she climbed up the staircase rising towards the turn at the top of the stairs. She would enter the bedroom and lay me down and then cover me with the blankets. I don't remember if she kissed me goodnight but I like to think she did.

When I am passing away I hope my mother will come for me. If she does, I will draw up my knees and close my eyes waiting for her to pick me up. If I feel her walking up the stairs with me in her arms I will feel warm and safe knowing that I am going to heaven.

***

'When you have a lot of problems first make a list of what's really important. Family and relationships first, work and money second and third. Ask what you can deal with now. Do them first and put the rest aside.

Add new things to the bottom of your list and make them wait. Take one problem at a time and then tick it off and go to number two.

***

***

Share your problems with other people who have had similar experiences. Make institutions wait for their money but talk to them. Pay your friends first.

Every time you tick off a problem no matter how small it will make you feel better.'

\*\*\*

**The twelve rules of a happy Christmas.**

On the first day of Christmas don't borrow any money.

On the second day of Christmas mute all TV advertising.

On the third day of Christmas put your phone on silent.

On the fourth day of Christmas go to a service and sing carols.

On the fifth day of Christmas remember 'peace and goodwill '.

On the sixth day of Christmas have a couple of drinks with your pals and sing.

On the seventh day of Christmas play a daft board game with the kids.

On the eight day of Christmas tell your family that you love them.

On the ninth day of Christmas take the dog for a walk.

On the tenth day of Christmas make a curry with the left-overs.

On the eleventh day of Christmas take a look at zero owing on your credit card.

On the twelfth day of Christmas go to sleep on the sofa and smile.

\*\*\*

'Dear God, this Christmas please make me as clever as all those people who know what the government should do.'

'No one remembers what their parents purchased for them, they remember the time they spent and with them.'

'My wife knows that I have the hearing abilities of a bat and I can see through walls. If I don't see or hear her it is because I am choosing to ignore what she is saying.'

\*\*\*

\*\*\*

'Don't tell people what they should have said - say it yourself.'

'If we spend all our time saving money we will fail to save our army, fail to save our culture and fail to save our country.'

When I go to heaven I want – pepper!

'Beware of charismatic puppets controlled by evil masters.'

\*\*\*

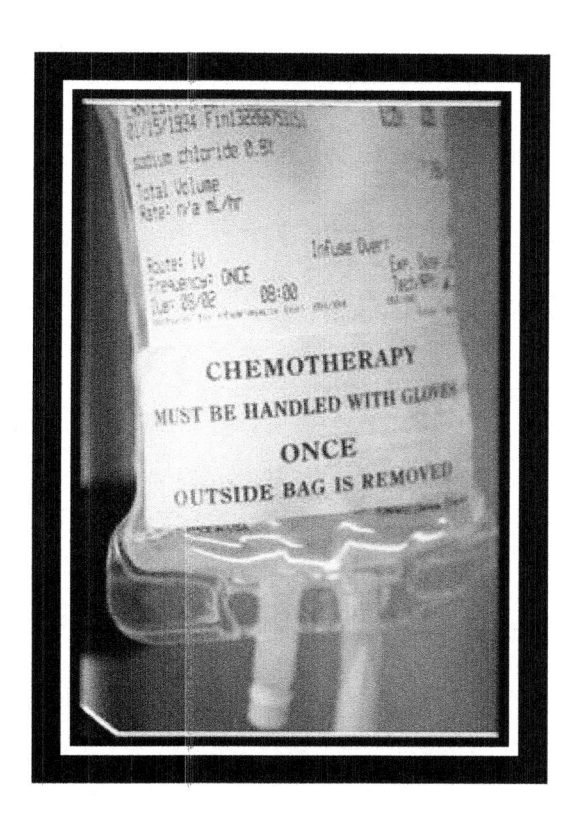

**Trip to Chemo'.**

Tired, the phone calls me from sleep

Sick, get dressed and catch a train

Walk, don't be sick, don't weep

Sit, while they fill my heart with poison

Wake, my veins have had their fill

Stand, in the queue, try not to swoon

Wait, for the girl with the pills

Swell, like a bloated balloon

Walk, and wait for the train

Sleep, don't sleep I'm feeling so weak

Sit, stand, walk and go home again

Suffer and go back next week.

\*\*\*

\*\*\*

'If the step from truth to plausible deniability is dangerous - how much worse is the next step - to implausible deniability?'

One way to lose all your friends and have a full time job is to start correcting their spelling on Facebook.

'People do not think in facts they think in emotions.'

\*\*\*

34

## **Everything I do.**

Everything I choose to do,

Everything I choose to say

Everything I have done

Everything I have ever said

Everything I will ever do, and

Everything I am going to say is

Not yours

Not theirs

Not ours

Not his or hers. It's

Mine, all mine

My responsibility!

***

'To obtain respect you must first be respectable.'

'There are no such people as 'they'.

'The most important and powerful word you ever learn is 'NO!'

'Those who have done nothing know everything.'

***

\*\*\*

'Humour should not be at the expense of someone else.'

'A friend in need is often in need of friends.'

'If you talk sense for long enough people will start to listen.'

'Ask not what I can do for you. Ask what you can do for yourself.'

\*\*\*

14 December 2018.

39

I am so pleased to hear that the advertising authorities are going to make greater efforts to avoid gender stereotyping.

At last we can see an end to advertisers portraying men as beer swilling, stupid, lazy people who need a substitute mother to keep them under control. We can see an end to humour that belittles men like 'Men behaving badly' and 'Doc Martin.'

No more laughing at the extremes of stupidity and farce that confronts us in normal life, no more ridiculing the differences between men and women. Now we can have a more puritanical society where all forms of masculinity can be held up as equal. A world where women can drink pints, swear, fart in public, get drunk in the streets and attack people is so much more desirable than the type of woman from my past.

They expected men to work all week while they managed the home. They wanted special bars to drink in (The Lounge), expected men to be polite in their company and open doors for them, to do the driving and to pay the bill on a date. In some cases wives took the week's wages and gave the men pocket money for the pub. Many a man crept home in fear of confronting his wife on the doorstep at midnight or spent the night on a friend's sofa for fear of personal injury. In those days hitting a woman under any circumstances was truly the worst of all crimes!

So thank God those days are over and we can all be equal in the eyes of the Independent Advertising Authority. I look forward to seeing their new sense of humour before I die of boredom or maybe I'll die because I just want to.

***

'A face mask converts a protestor into a rioter.'

'Cowards appear brave when they are winning.'

'Democracies love their leaders during war but despise them during peace.

'Arrogant winners are petulant losers.'

'If the BBC said Brexit would cause a nuclear

***

\*\*\*

war would you believe them and dig a shelter in the garden?'

'Throwing personal insults at your opponents does nothing to enhance your cause.'

'Leaders share their honour or their dishonour with their people.'

Nobody cares about the things you don't do.'

'Don't be a sympathyholic.'

\*\*\*

## A Soldier's Christmas Carol

A true story.

December found him embroiled in the endgame of a long war in Mozambique. The Russians had pulled out and left the war torn country to fend for itself. Nine months earlier along with other former British soldiers he had accepted the rank of Major in 'Frelimo', the Army of Mozambique.

That year had been a difficult one. The country was starving, foreign aid was pouring in but it never got to the interior unless it was in the hands of corrupt merchants who sold it at the local markets. There was no wildlife to eat it had all been wiped out by the nation's hungry people who were never short of an AK47 rifle and 7.62 ammunition. He had seen his soldiers die of malaria because they were on half rations. The food had been stolen before it got to the front line. One soldier who had been caught stealing food was ruthlessly whipped as punishment, when asked if it was worth it he said "Of course sir".

He looked forward to taking a break that Christmas, he couldn't go home to his own family until January, it wasn't his turn. His wife and three children would have to enjoy Christmas without him. His baby boy Oliver was only one year old and wouldn't notice but the other two were older Charlotte was six and Alex eight, it would affect them a lot. He missed them desperately but he was only doing the best to make a living he could the only way he knew.

The east coast of Africa was two hours drive away through enemy occupied territory but his fellow officer and friend Roger thought that making the trip on Christmas Eve would be worth the risk.

Roger knew of a store at the docks in Nacala where he could use their European cash to buy luxuries that they hadn't seen for some time.

They drove quickly and made the journey without encountering the enemy and arrived in time to fill a cold box with meat, ice, water, beer and champagne. Once the cold box was stored away safely for the next day they went to the old Portuguese Cathedral for the Christmas service. The church was full of worshippers but they felt uncomfortable dressed as they were, in uniform. In Africa in those days anyone in uniform was regarded with suspicion by friend and foe alike. They left the church and made plans to enjoy a private Christmas dinner for two on the beach the next day.

Waking late they drove the short distance to the coast where they found a fisherman who had caught a good sized Grouper which was excellent to eat. A little haggling and they had procured their meal for the day. Now they wondered where to go to cook it?

He drove the blue Safari Land Rover along the perfect, sandy beach until he found a lonely spot about twenty metres from the sea and sheltered by palm trees. There wasn't a soul in sight, a perfect place to barbeque the fish, drink the booze and relax away from the discomforts of war.

He began to hang his string hammock from the trees when the first local man arrived. The man made his greetings and asked for some water which was provided without quibble: it was the polite thing to do. Within minutes the empty beach began to fill with other people who all requested a share of his food. Although he did share, it became clear that if he didn't get stuck into his meal very quickly there wouldn't be much left. Becoming resentful he began opening the beer and drinking it quickly spilling it down his bare chest, he was tempted to tell them to go away. "Couldn't a man get one bloody day alone and eat his food without someone demanding a hand-out?"

He raised yet another beer to his lips and looked along the beach to see a little boy kicking a cheap plastic football. The boy was about two and a half, three at most and completely naked. A few feet away looking out at the sea sat the child's tired, young mother: she had the proud air of dignity. She had seen the worst of life and managed to survive. On her lap was a small parcel wrapped in newspaper. As he watched she opened the newspaper to reveal a small piece of bread and called out to the child. "At least somebody has brought something to the party" he mused.

Roger was busy cooking the Grouper on the barbeque surrounded by about six men who watched his every action with hungry anticipation. Roger seemed nonchalant and quite happy with their company. He however was not, he watched Roger and the revellers with a furrowed brow. The uninvited guests all had a beer now, his beer and it was clear that they were going to eat his Christmas Dinner. Anger welled up in his throat, just as he was about to speak up his attention was drawn downwards to a movement by his feet. There looking up at him was the little boy. In his right hand was the small piece of the bread his mother had given him. The child raised his tiny hand high above his head and offered to share the piece of bread. Smiling weakly he declined the generous offer and walked a few steps away to the beach to stare at the sea. Something in his throat wouldn't move, gradually he relaxed and took a deep breath holding his emotions in check. He brushed a tear from his cheek the way men do when they hope no one will notice.

The Dickensian message of Christmas had finally broken through.

***

'Man who makes personal remarks makes permanent enemies.'

'The University of Life and the University of Hard Knocks are offering a new degree. BA. DKH (ed. with Hons)'.

'While you are worrying about people who don't like you, they have gone fishing.'

Rude people have no defence against good manners.'

***

\*\*\*

'When you are powerless walk away and wait. Power flows - your day will come.'

'What does GOGG stand for? Grumpy Old Git Gift.'

'Could've, would've, should've are pointless.'

'Serious crime must result in serious punishment - the first time it happens.'

\*\*\*

54

## **Three on a bed.**

Grandma, daughter and granddaughter too

All snuggled together feeling so close

Watching Ru Paul who

Isn't that funny but - what do I know?

Three on a bed laughing and watching tv

Fluffy socks on toes with joyful, shiny cheeks

Laughing and smiling feeling so snuggly

The first time together for fifty-two weeks

Cognac and turkey and good music gives

A grandpa no space in this feminine place

I return to the room where the chocolate lives

Where I sit at the table and smile in good grace

*\*\*\**

\*\*\*

'The joy of life is associated with the risk of losing life.'

'Being seriously ill draws your family closer and drives your 'friends' further away.'

'In the 21st Century more than 80% of the world's population are going to die. More than 6 billion people………… fortunately 8 billion more will probably replace them.'

\*\*\*

***

'Hate isn't always a negative emotion. It sometimes keeps me going because I will never let that individual see me fail.'

'Spectators shouldn't tell players how to play.'

***

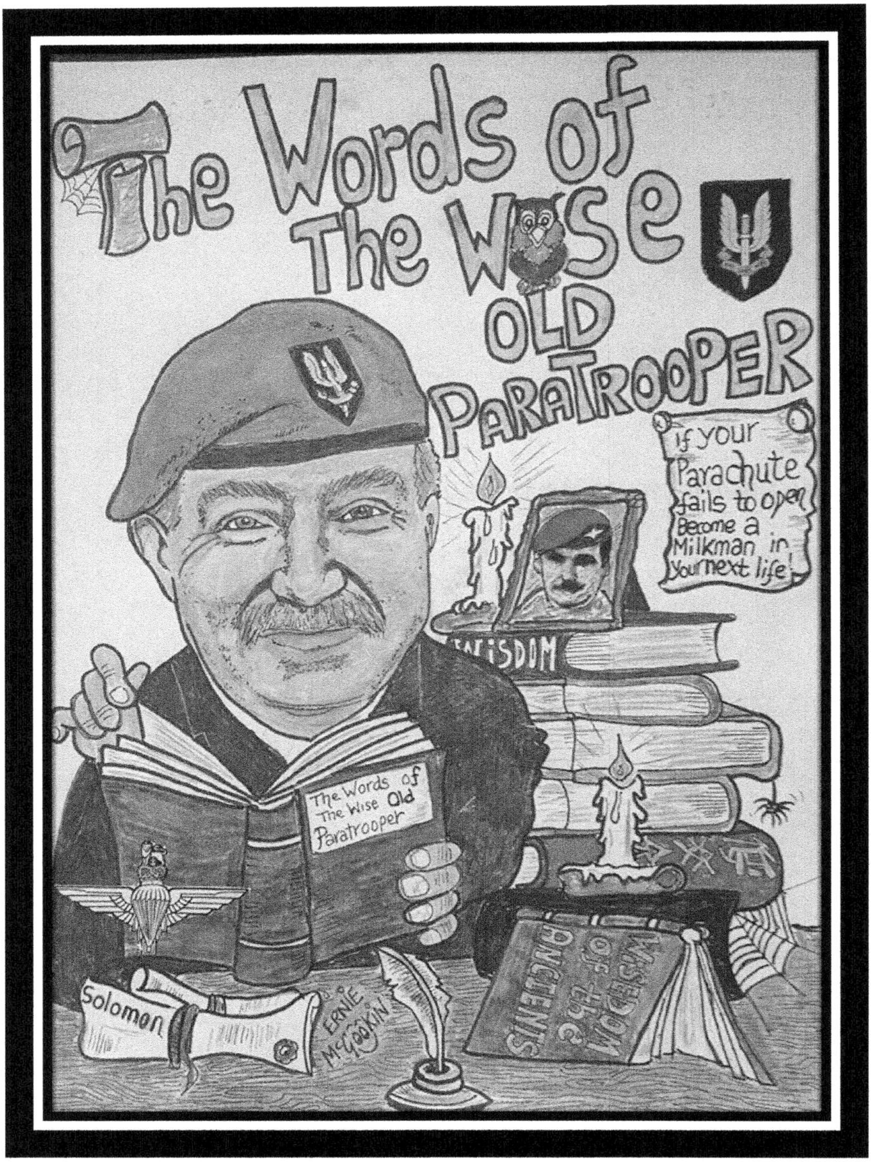
The Words of The Wise OLD PARATROOPER
If your Parachute fails to open Become a Milkman in Your next life!
WISDOM
The Words of The Wise Old Paratrooper
WISDOM OF THE ANCIENTS
Solomon
ERNIE McGOOKIN

**The Don'ts and Dos of the Wise Old Paratrooper.**

Don't run people down.

Don't be negative.

Don't judge others.

Don't make excuses for yourself.

Don't exaggerate.

Don't try to win other people's fights.

Don't intimidate.

Don't be dogmatic.

Don't let people antagonise you.

Don't complain for the sake of complaining.

Do say good things about people.

Do be optimistic.

Do be supportive of others.

Do accept that you get stuff wrong.

Do Stick to the verifiable truth.

Do fight your own battles.

Do be kind.

Do speak calmly but with passion.

Do be calm in an argument.

Do stop bloody moaning!

\*\*\*

'Desperate people tell desperate lies.'

'Sometimes it's hard to follow your own good advice.'

'Good parents train their kids for adulthood not perpetual childhood.'

'If you fall into bad company then you must be, - bad company.

\*\*\*

\*\*\*

'If academics only write and talk, tyrants don't care. Sometimes words are not enough.'

'Hiding shit behind the daisies doesn't get rid of the smell.'

'Optimists create change by trying, pessimists tell you you're doomed.'

'If you don't fight for right, eventually there will be no right.'

'Truth embarrasses the lie.'

\*\*\*

## In Slumber's Arms.

I sleep more now, my movement's slow

Only fingers, words and thoughts can race

Plato won his place o'er fertile love

Where I once led I must follow

I've lost my waking place.


I sleep more now, I hope to dream

Of times immortal, life long past

When happiness was one long day

Tomorrow could never come

Today would always, always last.


In dreams I run through storms of rain

With Hypnos I am young, happy!

In dreams there is no lingering pain

I sleep more now

In Slumber's arms - I'm free.

\*\*\*

'We miss them more as we get older.'

'When you break a window don't analyse it, don't convene a meeting, don't say 'lessons have been learned' - Just fix it!

'Once a man is a true man he will have his dignity, his integrity and his sense of decency. Many people will try to undermine those values with money, power and fame.'

\*\*\*

***

'A good story is always a good story. It doesn't need embellishing it just needs to be a good honest story and it will pass the test of time.'

'Don't confuse intellect with virtue it is a trick of the super and middle classes.'

***

**The Perfect Life.**

A man and his wife arrived at the gates of heaven. As they approached the pearly gates they were halted by St Peter who questioned them about their lives.

They informed St Peter that they had led good lives without sin of any kind. They had met when they were in their early twenties and they had lived strict religious lives, worked hard at school and never made time to play games or go on pointless adventures. They did go on educational expeditions where they learned about important facts that would be useful when they needed a job. They passed their examinations easily and went on to get Masters Degrees. During their education they never engaged in even the most minor sexual activity - they saved themselves for the night of their marriage.

Once married they earned good money and gave a percentage to charity every month, had two children and gave them the same good upbringing that they had received. They made sure their children were always safe and that they were never put at risk.

They were vegans never allowing meat or sugar to pass their lips and they never drank alcohol or experimented with drugs. They learned to dance so that they could participate on formal occasions but swore that they never really enjoyed the activity. Music of certain types were allowed provided that were acceptable to their social group. Good, clean, high-brow, *approved* melodies.

They saved their money and never had to ask another human being for help. Their money was put into investments and savings for the time when they grew old.

Their children grew up and for reason they couldn't comprehend their offspring left home and only visited once a year with their children. This was a relief as the noise of children and the break in routine was upsetting. No matter how good they were they could not persuade their children to mimic their proven path to success. Their children were a disappointment.

In old age they had doctors who kept them both alive until they were over one hundred years old. Their medical insurance paid for operations, drugs, potions and treatments that extended their lives so far that they outlived their offspring. They died within moments of one another by arrangement with their physicians. Euthanasia – it was all very civilised. They planned it as they had planned all of their life, even to the point of rehearsing for this moment should it happen.

St Peter listened carefully and asked them to wait while he checked inside. A short time later he returned and informed them that there was no place in heaven for them but equally there was no place in hell. They could remain in purgatory as ghosts or return to the world of life to try again at being good people.

The couple asked for an explanation citing their story and reminding St Peter of their almost perfect lives. 'What possible reason could God have for rejecting us' asked the woman?

Peter explained that during his absence he had taken their story to The Lord and had received the following explanation.

He explained that God gave them gifts they rejected. How would they feel if they gave a child a bicycle and the child refused to ride it? God their father had provided healthy bodies and intelligent minds, he had given them pleasures in sex, love, food, laughter, companionship, music and dance and they had refused them – all on the grounds that they wanted to be safe and live perfect lives.

He went on, 'You rejected life, and you rejected God's gifts - because of this you had one hundred years without life. You both treated life as a test of how perfect you could be instead of a test of how much better you could be. You didn't test how fast you could run, how far you could fall and rise up. You should have sung the songs and danced for the pure joy of dancing. You should have let your children do the same but you protected them from life and eventually they rejected you. You wasted your lives. Living in sin' he said 'is not the same as living without joy.'

As they left they looked back and from the far side of the gates two figures came into view and sadly waved goodbye --- it was their children.

***

\*\*\*

'Give yourself the same advice you would give a friend.'

'Learn from the past and improve your future.'

'If you dig down past lies, opinions and beliefs you might just find a nugget of truth.'

'Do not turn an act of kindness into a loan.'

'I was only saying' doesn't cut it.'

'Train to be an employer not an employee.'

\*\*\*

**Broad Wings.**

When will I see your like again

We'll never share another day

Time will take us all

Our friendship and pride

Will overcome the pain

This moment was a fleeting day

On Pegasus' broad wings

Charged with history

From a bygone youth

Five thousand Spartan brothers in

Our welded bond of love.

77

more words
of the
Wise Old
Paratrooper
BY
ROBIN
HORSFALL
ERNIE
McGOOKIN
FIGHTING
SCARED
ROBIN
HORSFALL

**Rhetorical Questions!**

If people protest about violence by damaging property are they being violent?

If I punish a violent person with violence will I teach them that violence has no place in society?

If I punish a criminal by being kind will I make the criminal kinder?

If people have mental health issues and make other people depressed with their behaviour does this mean that mental health issues are infectious?

If laughter make us laugh is laughter infectious?

If I allow everyone to drink alcohol will everyone become an alcoholic?

If I allow everyone to take drugs will everyone become an addict?

If I tell everyone what they want to hear will they all like me?

If I tell everyone the truth will they all like me?

If I stop asking difficult questions will you all applaud?

***

'Being honest about your dishonesty doesn't make you more honest.'

'If you need to know how you truly feel about someone imagine them dead tomorrow.'

'If you think the world is a mess don't just throw insults and complain, try to change it.'

***

***

'When you judge others be aware of how your judgement affects you.'

'The stupid queue doesn't get shorter with time.'

'Dissident, Republican Splinter Group' can be translated as 'IRA.'

'The consequences of remaining silent against tyranny are dreadful.'

***

\*\*\*

'It's not always someone else's fault. Sometimes it's just life.'

'If a home is where the heart is, my life is where my wife is.'

'Most people remember the first and the last thing you say - the rest is just ssssssssss'

'If we want freedom of speech we shouldn't use words as assault weapons.'

\*\*\*

***

'Excellence of performance produces success, - excellence of spirit produces happiness.'

'We must teach our children and our students to be better than we are.'

'In a random group of fifty people there are – one bully, one hero, one victim and forty-eight watchers.'

***

## **The King of the Chimps**

A thousand years ago in darkest Africa the men lived on the ground while the Chimpanzees lived in the trees.

One day the King of the Chimps who was named Ogi went to the King of Men, 'Igo' and asked for an audience which was granted.

'Come and be our King for a while' suggested Ogi. 'Come and teach us how to be men so that we can come down from the trees and be more like you. Teach us how to make fire and spears so that we can eat well and be warm at night.'

Igo considered the request and after much consideration agreed. During his deliberations he decided that extending his influence into the high trees and ruling the Chimps would make him a more powerful king.

A few days later Igo arrived in the forest and gave his first commands. 'I have three requests if you are to learn to be men.

First you must stop screaming at one another.

Second you must stop hitting one another.

Third you must all shit at the edge of your territory, not in the group area.'

Ogi happily agreed and passed the command onto his group.

A short time later two females were heard screaming. They were called upon to answer for their behaviour.

Igo asked;

Why were you screaming? –

She was looking at my mate –

Why is that a problem? –

I have a good mate and she wants to steal him. –

Why did you scream at her? –

I wanted to hit her but you said we can't do that so it was easier to scream . I have a good mate and she was flirting with him. –

Don't you trust your mate? –

Of course not! –

Couldn't you ignore her? –

No. It's too much hard work to be quiet when someone wants to take my mate. Screaming at her works.

The King of Men contemplated and sent them away.

A short time later a fight began between two males. They were called to answer for their behaviour.

Igo asked;

Why did you fight? –

He was disrespecting me and getting in my space? –

Is that a good reason to fight? –

Yes if I allow him to do that he will take my place and my mates. –

Why don't you just tell him that you will fight him if he doesn't go away? -

You told us not to scream. It's hard work not screaming when you are angry and even harder not to fight. Anyway screaming and fighting is what we do and it works.

The King of men contemplated and sent them away.

The following morning a family was seen shitting from the branches into the group territory. They were called upon to answer for their actions.

Igo enquired of their reasons.

'It's too much hard work walking down the tree and all the way to the edge of our lands just to have a shit. It's much simpler to just wake up and shit on everything below.'

Ogi the King of Chimps looked at the King of Men and shrugged. They both knew it wasn't going to work.

Igo set off on the long walk home, he was disappointed in the Chimps, he had held such great hopes.

'Ah well' he said 'At home I can't stop them screaming or fighting either but at least I can get everyone to shit in the right place.

Moral: It's the little things that make us different.

## The Blanket

What makes you truly happy? Winning some money, seeing an enemy defeated, getting a pay rise? I don't mean the sort of happy created by a good laugh or getting a good joke. I mean the sort of moment that makes you tingle inside, sometimes to the point of tears when you feel so connected to someone that for a moment in time you are truly fulfilled.

It is my experience that these moments are always created by the emotion we weakly describe as love. It happens to me when my

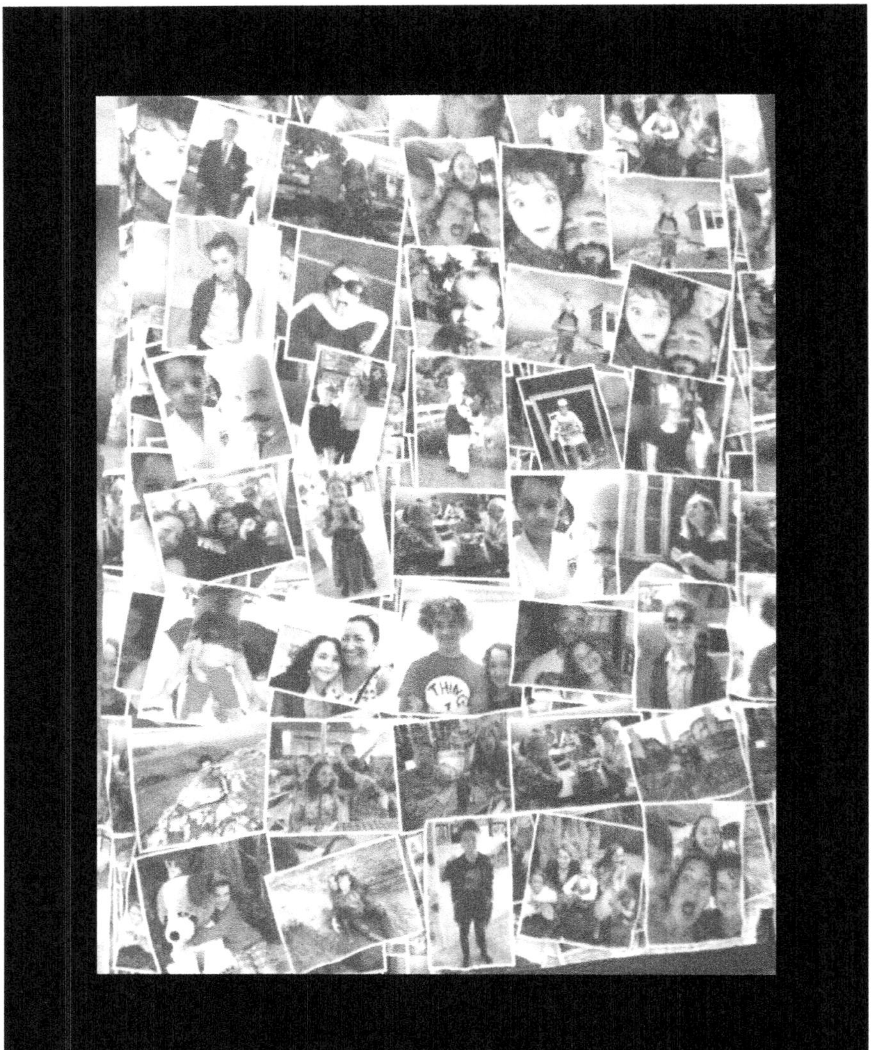

family shows a deep concern for my welfare with meaningful gestures. The gestures are never large or exaggerated, in fact sometimes I have to stop for a moment to realise that they happened. A hug, a touch, an embarrassed word, a card with kisses or the offer of a sweet have all made me want to hold onto that moment for a while. I know how rare and valuable these moments are, so I don't release them too quickly. This doesn't embarrass me but I often walk away and hide my face for fear of being observed as far too happy.

At Christmas I received a blue blanket with pictures of my family printed on the surface. Lots of my kids and grandkids smiling and laughing at me. You might ask why a blanket with photos on it was going to be so important and why it could move me so much?

Well, the following week I went into hospital for a radical cystectomy to treat my bladder cancer. For two weeks that blanket laying on my bed was their way of holding my hand. They wanted to be with me and that very thought and gesture made me -------- well it just did, okay?

\*\*\*

'If you want to save people get them to think.'

'Our government will only believe that we need a strong army when someone else starts a war.'

'I love meals where I get to see a tyrant eat Pelosi pie.'

'The only way to defeat a bully is to fight back and then fight back again and then fight back again and ...'

\*\*\*

\*\*\*

'When a population is persuaded that all violence is wrong that population will become noisy, complaining and frightened slaves to their government.'

'Anger is often extinguished by the words of a wise friend.'

\*\*\*

**Sniper fear.**

In 1983 I was part of a British Army Training Team in Salalla in the south of Oman. My troops were Baluchi from the south of Pakistan.

They were among the most reliable and courageous troops in SOAF the Sultan of Oman's Armed Forces.

Given a great deal of freedom the Baluchi Colonel asked me to provide a snipers course for his troops. I spent the next two weeks acquiring ranges, equipment, weapons and writing the course. It was based on the Royal Marine Sniper Course that I had completed in 1982.

The day dawned the troops assembled outside the barracks to start the course. 'Sergeant

Horsfall' the Colonel's voice came from off to the side. 'Send the men back to barracks please. Perhaps we could have a word.'

The course was cancelled at the command of the Sultan of Oman. The Sultan didn't want snipers in the Baluchi forces. Leaders of countries are more frightened of assassination by sniper than any other method. The leaders of the world live in fear of us.

\*\*\*

'If all our problems could be cured by violence we would have run out of problems a long time ago.'

'Only after the birth of your first child can you truly understand how much your parents love you.'

'Everyone has the right to speak their mind but everyone else has the right not to listen, not to agree and sometimes to vehemently disagree!'

'If you always assume the worst about people you will rarely be disappointed but you will never achieve anything.'

'There is no benefit getting straight to the point if you can't get your audience to listen.'

\*\*\*

**A visit to Trumpton the home of homonyms.**

Last knight I went to Whales to meet the Prints of wails. I had an amazing talk with some very good people I no about there nights in shinning amour. In the mourning I had a very good brake fast of eggs and bake on. By lunch thyme I was beginning to tyre and Wayne. Have ewe herd that the Universe city of Cardiff are going to give me an honorary doctor rate in my own language - American. I'm a stable genius'.

102

## Rough Men

Rough men taught me a lot

Clever men taught me to think

Stupid men taught me cruelty

Foolish men taught me to laugh

Angry men taught me to be careful

Good men taught me courage

Quiet men taught me respect

Brave men taught me to say 'no'.

Mannered men taught me dignity

My wife taught me kindness and love.

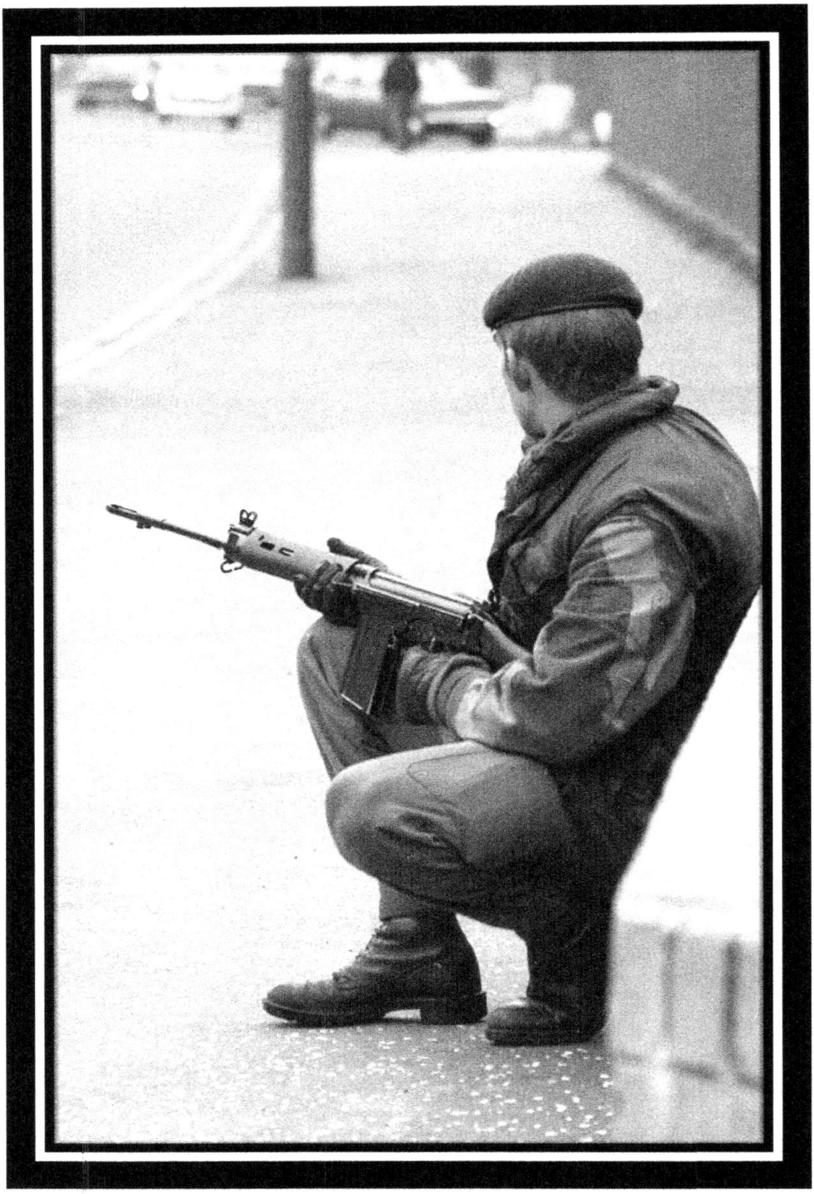

## Gone.

The things we used to do

That no one else knew

No longer count as true

The acts for friendship's sake

Without a PC brake.

The things we used to do

That no one else knew

No longer count as true.

The joy of playing war

Practised violence for

Our youthful days of yore.

*\*\**

\*\*\*

'Give a boy responsibility and he will be productive.'

'Boys are aggressive give them an enjoyable outlet for that aggression'

'It isn't war that creates PTSD, it is exile from the security of military life.'

\*\*\*

***

'Saying 'no' is quick way of discovering who a new colleague really is.'

'When you cheat Death you only get to play a few more hands before losing.'

'Live not in fear of what might come but in fear of what is here and now and fight!'

***

**Golden Memories.**

Music holds my memories and holds my heart.

A Hard Days Night in the pool in sixty-four with mum

Delila on Top-of the-Pops with Tom in black and white

Laying in fear from Doctor Who tubular bells and a guitar drum

San Francisco and Mony Mony in German streets

The 66 world cup with Tommy James and the Shondells

Riding on the fair with mayonnaise and frits

Music holds my history music holds my heart

Woodstock and school to escape from it all

Blockbuster made my bedroom sound Sweet

Mungo In the Summetime laying by Aldershot pool

Even David Essex was gonna Rock on which was neat

10 CC told me that big boys don't cry, I was so shy

A last dance at disco to the voice of Barry White

Walking girls back home hoping for a season in the sun

Music is my story music fills my heart

Taking the long walk alone ain't so heavy, he's my brother

Dreaming of Anje and hoping for our Waterloo

Ground Control called Major Tom as a young soldier

111

My story is my music my memories too

Ian Hit me with his rhythm stick in the David Garrick

The Drury was out and The Police fought the Blockheads

I fell in love and it made us made us Move Closer

It was the end of Girls, Girls, Girls and a lot of Moonlight

We didn't need a Donna to sing for us that Summer

Nights in White Satin turned darkness to light.

It Hurt so Good that I danced myself dizzy and Bonnie called

For a Hero to put all the wrongs right.

Ave Maria holds my day in Church while Billy sang

D_I_V_O_R_C_E to his dog but Tammy told her

To stand by her man cos Breaking up is very hard to do

Music holds my history and makes my senses purr.

Walking on eighties beaches I didn't like Mondays

I didn't get the meanings of 'Peaches' and Roxy

Took a Chance on me as I left for war in S_A.

A child is born while The Ant sung Friend from Foe.

The Power of Love when far from home caused a hush

Pavarotti in Africa playing opera while the people fast

Lost and empty alone listening to Jennifer Rush.

Music holds my dreams my passage to the past

It's all there with Elton and Cat and Carly and Wham

My sister said 'Your so Vain' but the song was about me

So she sent in the clowns to stifle the young man

This music is my history from zero to sixty

A Bitter Sweet Symphony brought me home

No more Guns and Roses behind the Wonderwall

B52s would no longer roar and roam - no longer alone

Music is my history, music knows it all.

\*\*\*

'A quick way to lose friends is by correcting their spelling on Facebook.'

'Winning a medal requires a fortunate moment and an enthusiastic Commanding Officer.'

'A moment of courage doesn't a hero make.'

\*\*\*

\*\*\*

'Reasonable disagreement makes you a thinker, crude disparagement just makes you vulgar.'

'When you have children you will understand how your parents feel about you.'

'Ideas compete, people are just their tools.'

\*\*\*

## More Rules of the Wise Old Paratrooper.

1. Stop whining, everyone has problems.

2. If your life is going wrong start to fix it.

3. Don't rely on drink and drugs, they don't improve anything.

4. Tell the truth all the time.

5. Be happy for the success of others.

6. Only talk about people you like.

7. Keep your promises especially to your wife and kids.

8. Only keep company with decent, positive people.

9. Be a good example all of the time.

10. Start today!

***

***

'Don't takes a well-intentioned statement and corrupt it with a different meaning.'

'When you've lived long enough, done enough and seen enough, you know that most of your 'enough' was nearly all just fun and games.'

***

\*\*\*

'If you allow gangsters to stop you from speaking out, if you spend your life trying not to be noticed by the bullies, if you don't stand up for the truth, then you will have no place in decent society because decent society will not exist.'

'Never mind saying 'They should' or 'We should' or 'Someone should'. Start saying 'I will', 'I'm going to' and 'I will start to fight.'

'Teach ethics before mathematics.'

\*\*\*

## Mercurial Bill

Bill was probably as messed up as me at the age of fifteen. Sometimes he was my pal and other times my worst enemy. Mercurial might be an appropriate description of his character.

In October 1972, we were all fifteen-year-old recruits at the Infantry Junior Leaders Battalion in Oswestry, Shropshire. We were divided into regimental platoons. Bill, me and the rest of our platoon were Paras with a couple of Light Infantrymen for seasoning and in the barrack block adjoining ours were the Guards, - our arch rivals.

We shared an ablution block that joined our barracks together. As a result we washed, shaved, cleaned and ironed our clothes in a shared space.

About six weeks into our recruit course Bill had an altercation with a tall, fair, handsome young

Guardsman. He stood a good three inches taller than Bill, so Bill compensated by picking up the steam iron to use as a weapon.

As we watched, Bill launched himself towards his adversary and tried to swing the iron but found himself standing back where he started with a surprised look on his face. The Guardsman had taken up a boxing stance with his feet well set and his hands held ready.

Bill advanced again with the same result a sharp, straight jab hit him smack in the face and he bounced away again. Unperturbed he tried several more times without any positive effect. He was still on his feet, which was creditable but I think the boxer was playing with him. Bill finally let his arms drop to his sides and walked away past his audience into the safety of our barrack block, bewildered and defeated.

***

***

'Grown-ups are supposed to be grown up.'

'It's no good keeping account for our money if we can't stay in credit with our behaviour.'

'When I lied all the time they made me their leader. When I lied some of the time they said 'To err is to be human' and forgave me. When I never lied and defended the truth they crucified me.

***

***

'Don't ask what you have done - ask what you have achieved.'

'Hate is not a human need.'

'In my next life I want to be really stupid. People will be kinder and if they are not I won't know. I will probably be happier.'

***

## The Proud Old General.

Oh great General Priapus

How proud you stood

In helmeted glory

To firmly refuse the flow

Of all who dared to stand before you

Even Venus' fair lips that parted

And welcomed you

Grew tired and worn

At your refusal to stand down

When surging passions flowed

Did you resist and

Show your manly pride

But now old King

Where once great forces stood

You may sleep your rest

And stand proud no more.

\*\*\*

***

'Everyone hears a quiet, old dog when he barks.'

'Power only retreats from a greater power!'

'We learn best by trying, failing and trying again.'

'A Doctor can extend your life but no one can save it.'

'The first hiding place of a fool is behind an insult.'

\*\*\*

\*\*\*

'Martial Arts' is two words. The first is related to fighting the second to cultural and philosophical development. With the first you learn to fight, - add the second and the fighter learns to become a better human being.'

'You can't give someone flowers when they are shooting at you.'

\*\*\*

***

'I wrote things down for people who couldn't listen - then I discovered that they couldn't read either.'

'There are two universal laws. Don't start fights and don't take people's stuff.'

'You can't lose what you don't value.

***

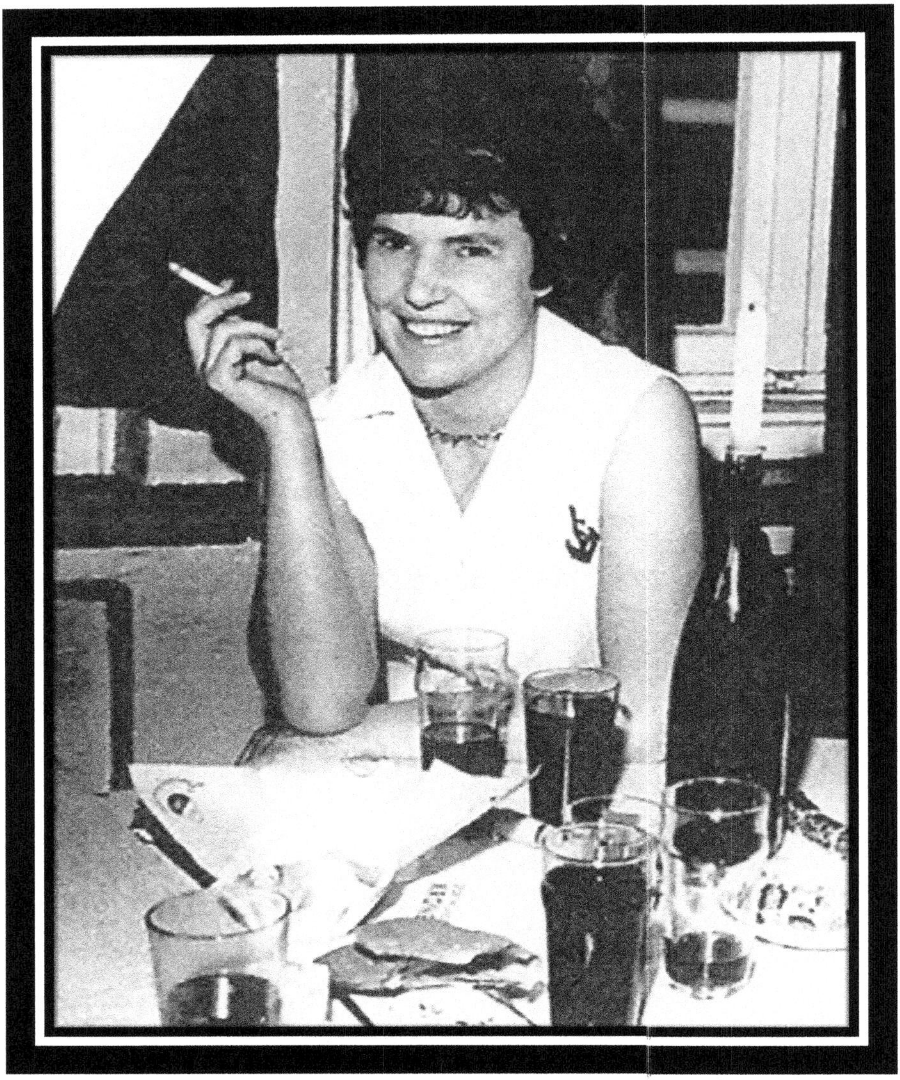

## **Love Unspoken**

When you left us you were very young

Your love was rarely spoken

Mother you left an ancient song

Of care, and heart, and love unbroken

I held the pram you pushed for miles

Your love was rarely spoken


And held your hand and walked to school

With care and heart, and love unbroken.

I held you tight, embraced and waved farewell

Your love was rarely spoken

Departing from the place we dwelt

From care and heart, and love unbroken.


I wasn't there to thank you and say goodbye

Our love was rarely spoken

All night , all night in tears I cried

My care and heart and love -- now spoken.

\*\*\*

'If you agree with everything someone says you are probably deaf!'

'Silence is a useful weapon against fools - but it has its limits'.

'Give the most to the one who needs the most.'

\*\*\*

***

Wees Old Porotraper says 'Read what you write before you post it.'

'You can't respect someone for speaking their mind and then disrespect their opponents for doing the same.'

***

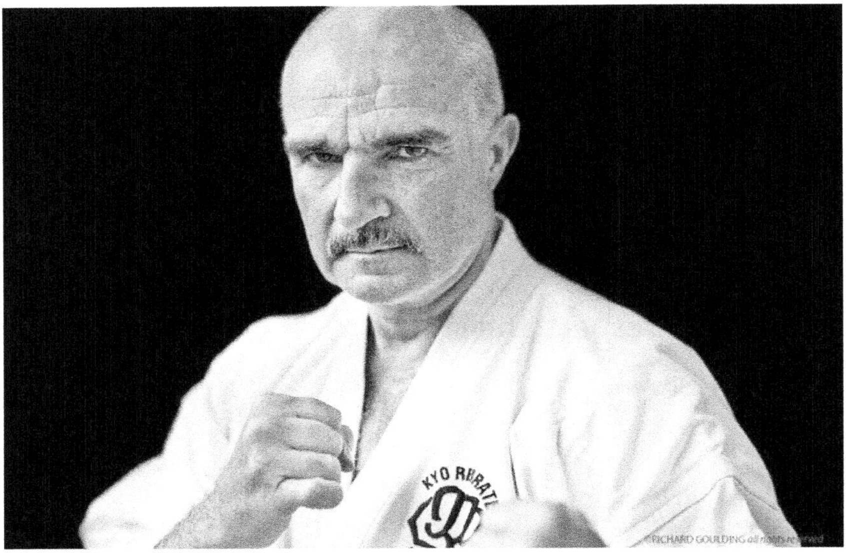
KYO RKRATE
©RICHARD GOULDING all rights reserved

**I'D RATHER**

I'd rather be good than evil.

I'd rather assist than turn away.

I'd rather give than deny.

I'd rather peace than war.

I'd rather talk than fight.

I'd rather love than hate.

I'd rather you didn't push your luck!

138

## Bears in the Woods.

In 1977 X&Y Vigilant Platoons were the wild bunch of the Parachute Regiment. A specialist anti-tank guided missile group they were completely independent of the battalions. They had their own budget and their own vehicles. The troops were older than average and usually had spent three years with a battalion before going to 'Vig'. They prided themselves on their fitness, their wildness and their awesome singing abilities.

A superb trip was planned to Canada in 1977 which included live firing of missiles, a trip to the rodeo and some climbing in the Rockies. Paratroopers have very little respect for anything including their own lives. This disrespect is enhanced by alcohol but there was one thing that everyone in Canada had respect for - Grizzly bears.

Whenever anyone was out in the wild the message was always make a noise, let them know you are there, play dead if you are caught and so on.

After returning from the hills one day the men sat down around a fire and proceeded to celebrate, there was no shortage of wine and song. In the early hours the troops gradually faded away back to their cabins while some chose to stay out under the starts in their sleeping bags.

One man who had drunk more than his share of booze curled up in his green maggot (sleeping bag) for the night at the foot of a tree.

In the morning a boot roused him and a voice asked 'Where did all this shit come from?' His face slowly emerged from the bag and he pulled down the zip. A hangover was emerging with him and his eyes slowly focused as he tried to make sense of the question.

He was covered in tree bark. Above him were the huge claw marks where a Grizzly had sharpened its claws while he slept.

***

'When a man is truly tired he looks old.'

'If you are a bully and your parents are not ashamed of you then you should be ashamed of your parents.'

'People with too much time on their hands are very easily offended.'

***

\*\*\*

'There are two essential qualities in a decent man - Courage and Compassion.'

'Following the opinions of the masses is only an M away from the truth.'

'If you don't know what to say a look of compassion or a touch on the shoulder carries just as much meaning.'

\*\*\*

***

'Some men are led into battle – the rest are fed into battle.'

'Tough men don't need to talk tough.'

'Admiring the physical qualities of opposite sex is not sexist!'

'Doing things for our kids denies them the opportunity to learn and do it for themselves.'

'Those who set high personal standards are often abused by those with the opposite.'

***

146

**They love you now.**

Lonely boy, unpopular child

How lost you were

Without a friend

They love you now

In their thousands

But you can't love them back

You know who they are

And remember.

**Dominant Species?**

It was a relief to feel gravity again, I had been in

space stasis for some time in liquid form. The

transformation was wonderful, I was mobile, I could feel and consume nourishment.

My mission in this solar system was to identify the dominant species on the third planet from the star. It was essentially a water planet but it teemed with life. It was hard to know where to start, - the obvious place would have been in the water had it not been for the myriad energy sources that emanated from the land masses.

My investigations showed that there was a bipedal humanoid that appeared to be the species responsible for all of this technology, so I decided to observe them first.

I descended to those sites that I had identified with energy supply. The technology was primitive relying on decaying radioactivity or even fossil fuels. Small number of humanoids or humans as they call themselves operated vast energy production centres. There were other species present but they seemed insignificant to the humans. Six-legged insects were the most prevalent but there was very little interaction between the two groups. Perhaps size played a part.

I moved to the places of maximum human population and descended into the recreational areas called 'Parks'. As I observed, I noticed that humans to indeed interact with other species. I watched a large number of humans escorting canine quadrupeds. This was not an isolated case, during my travels I observed the same interaction on all the land masses and in all the cities.This symbiosis of the two creatures interested me. They seemed to be dependent on one another.

I had up to this point surmised that the humans were the dominant species. They controlled the food supply, the energy, manufacturing, transport and trade between different groups but something troubled me with this conclusion.

As my studies continued I discovered that the canines were in fact one species. They were all descended from an ancestor known as a wolf. The wolf still exists in remote areas but has little or no interaction with humans. It is a clever, social beast but in the distant past the humans gained superior technology and hunted it almost to extinction.

It appears that the wolves countered this genocide by giving their young to the humans to be trained as guards and hunting companions. This cooperation was successful, however, the humans knew that the wolves were strong, clever and dangerous. By a process of selective breeding they made the wolf less aggressive and encouraged traits that were identified with pups rather than adults. The new subservient animal was called 'a dog'.

Oppressed, controlled and deprived of their freedom the dogs spent many generations as the slaves of the humans. However, my recent studied made me realise that something had changed since this oppression began.

I watched the humans as they walked in the park with their dogs. The human was attached to the dog with a piece of rope and it was clear in most cases that the human was walking and stopping at the command of the dog. Frequent stops occurred for the dog to urinate and indicate to other dogs that it had been there. It was a wonderful conversation with hundreds of dogs saying 'I'm here, I've been here, I'm looking for a mate' and so on. The humans seemed oblivious of the noise that was reverberating around them and constantly looked at an amusement device that was permanently attached to one hand. This item appeared to distract the humans while the dogs investigated the depths of their interaction.

I realised that the Park was not a recreational area for humans but it was in fact a toilet for dogs. Every time a dog defecated a human would obediently clean up the dog's faeces, place it in a bag and transport it to a local receptacle for other humans to remove. Some of the dogs were shy and unhappy with this arrangement and didn't like to be observed so they would conceal themselves between parked cars or wait until the humans weren't paying attention and then leave their toilet for another human to discover. The park/toilet was generally clean thanks to the human slaves.

Humans have their own children who receive great comfort from soft warm toys. The wolves of yesteryear had been clever, they had left instructions, behave like a human child and when you breed look for traits that make you look like a human toy. So, the dogs got smaller, developed false smiles and longer hair. They maintained their puppy behaviour but I came to the conclusion that unbeknown to the humans the dogs had taken control.

If a slave (human) grew frustrated with the needs of their masters they would often pull against their ropes or make loud aggressive noises. To regain control of their disobedient slaves the dogs would simply pretend to be puppies or furry toys. In response to this the human would make strange gurgling noises and groom its master. Order was quickly restored.

As I watched in became clear, the humans would rise from sleep in the morning and prepare food for the dog, the dog would remain in the bed that he allowed the human to share when the food was ready. Only then could the slaves prepare food for themselves and their offspring.

Although the house was built and furnished by the humans the dog was the owner, it could take food from the humans, destroy the furnishing and control the sleeping arrangements of the family. If the dog wanted to leave the property it would threaten and snarl or even defecate in the human rest areas to obtain whatever it desired.

When a slave was large and the dog small, the dog would often refuse to walk insisting on being carried in a basket draped over the human's shoulder. The dog would be transported from meeting to meeting and only descend for food, toilet or grooming.

I was intrigued by how masterful the dogs were. The humans obtained great status from the size and shapes of their masters. Humans would often labour for many hours to obtain enough credit to become the slave of an unborn dog. The more they paid for their future master the more status they obtained among their human peer group. Great verbal whoops of admiration would greet a new master when other slaves came to pay homage.

A dog would be cherished from birth, fed without the need for labour, carried and groomed and do as it pleased, when it pleased and with whomever it pleased.

The day of the dog was clearly upon this planet. It was the dominant species!

161

***

\*\*\*

'If you want to be a hero - love your wife, support your family and set a good example to your kids. You will be a hero to them and that's all that counts.'

'If you can't please all the people all of the time, then please your own people. If you can't please them then please the good people and if you can't please them - then sod it - please yourself.'

\*\*\*

***

'If you preach you had better be as good as your words.'

'The difference between successful people and the rest is the ability to keep going, not to give in, not to whine and to find a way to succeed.'

***

My Nature - A Moment Of Introspection.

'I like being a man.' That sounds fine doesn't it?

I think it's a safe thing to say about myself 'I like being a man.' -

Do you think there is something wrong with that statement? -

Well, it's a safe thing for me to say in contemporary society if I refuse to elaborate but it's dangerous if I allow someone with what I regard as an extremist agenda to deconstruct my sentence. -

What do you mean by claiming that you like being a man? Does it mean you don't like women? -

Of course it means nothing of the sort but by simply asking the question you imply that I might not like women. It isn't an inference because it isn't an educated guess it is a subliminal suggestion, the planting of a false idea perhaps even the planting of a rumour. -

So what do you mean when you say you like being a man? -

Well, one part of my answer would be that I like being masculine. I like competing in a physical and academic environment. I like challenging authority, I like singing loud songs. I used to like a fight, sometimes a training fight and sometimes a real fight. I like feeling powerful and I like to celebrate my nature. You might ask whether I dislike femininity. -

Do you dislike femininity? -

I don't understand why liking sugar means that I hate salt. I like my masculinity and I also like femininity particularly in the case of the opposite sex. I have always been attracted to feminine women. -

So, does that mean that you only like feminine women.-

No, I like lots of women but I am only attracted to feminine women. -

Does that mean you are homophobic? -

No, I like lots of different people and I dislike lots of different people, including some feminine women – but I find feminine women attractive.-

Isn't being masculine according to your criteria dangerous and threatening? -

Yes if it is tyrannical but no if you want to be protected from a tyrant. -

What do you mean by feminine?-

Difficult question and a dangerous one. I like women who have most of the feminine strengths, the ability to manage emotional difficulty, the freedom to be gentle without being weak, the ability to enchant and to soften the extremes of masculinity, the ability to make men feel proud and ashamed. -

Whoa stop! You said 'particularly in the case of the opposite sex' right isn't that statement homophobic? –

No, I don't think so. I'm not attracted to men I'm a profound heterosexual so although I like some feminine men I do not desire them. I never have and I never will, this is my nature. I like my nature, I like me, I like being a heterosexual and masculine man. -

Ah but that's not what you said at the start. –

I know, this is what I meant when I questioned myself by saying 'I think it's a safe thing to say about myself'. Now however, I have to be careful, because simply by liking my own nature I leave myself open to questions that suggest that my nature is in some way corrupt, anachronistic or even wicked. –

Is it? -

No it isn't. My masculinity is normal and healthy, my wife loves my masculinity even though at times she has found a need to control my excesses, in particular my temper. For forty years she has found my nature attractive. She has never been my physical equal - I am by nature much bigger and stronger than she is and as a result I always felt a duty to protect her. She on the other hand has a superior emotional intelligence and has used that to protect me. She has controlled me with her femininity which is an adjunct to her wisdom. –

Healthy? –

Yes my masculinity combined with her femininity allowed us to produce a well-balanced and long lasting relationship.

So what did you really mean to say then? -

I suppose I really meant to say 'I'm a male, masculine, heterosexual and I really, really do like being that way. -

Hmmm.

Wise Old Paratrooper says 'Get married young and have kids. Give your family at least a third of your time, grow up together as they grow up. Love your marriage partner especially when they drive you nuts. Begin every day as though yesterday never happened. Always sleep in a double bed. Grow old without being lonely.'

175

Endex

## Other books by Robin Horsfall

*Fighting Scared (2002)*

*The Words of the Wise Old Paratrooper (2017)*

*More Words of the Wise Old Paratrooper (2018)*

www.wiseoldparatrooper.co.uk

Printed in Great Britain
by Amazon